Speedy Handwriting practice for Year 2!

When it comes to Handwriting, practice is key — and this CGP book is packed with speedy workouts for every week of Year 2!

Each workout has a mixture of activities matched to the National Curriculum. Use them for starter activities, recaps, homework tasks... or any way that suits you!

We've even included extra challenges and handy progress charts. Ace!

Published by CGP
ISBN: 978 1 83774 205 9

Editors: Emma Duffee, Raya Milushev, Kirsty Sweetman

With thanks to Aimee Ashurst and Juliette Green for the proofreading.

With thanks to Beth Linnane for the copyright research.

Images throughout the book © Educlips 2025

Printed by Elanders Ltd, Newcastle upon Tyne.

Based on the classic CGP style created by Richard Parsons.

Text, design, layout and original illustrations
© Coordination Group Publications Ltd. (CGP) 2025
All rights reserved.

Photocopying this book is not permitted, even if you have a CLA licence.
Extra copies are available from CGP with next day delivery • 0800 1712 712 • www.cgpbooks.co.uk

How to Use this Book

- This book contains 36 workouts. We've split them into 3 sections, one for each term, with 12 workouts each. There's roughly one workout for every week of the school year.
- Each workout should take about 10 minutes. There's a self-assessment box at the end of each workout for pupils to track their confidence.
- Each workout starts with a warm-up question and ends with a fun puzzle.
- The first 2 workouts recap the alphabet, capital letters and numbers. The rest of the Autumn Term introduces joined-up writing and break letters. Pupils then practise the joins between letters by tracing and copying words and sentences.
- Progress charts can be found at the back of the book.
- If you are a parent or guardian using this book at home with your child, bear in mind that different schools have different handwriting styles. Some schools also have different break letters (letters that don't join to the next letter). For example, 'g' can be a break letter or it can be joined. You should check with the school to see how each letter is written.

The contents page will help you identify the focus of each workout. You can use this to pick the workout that best suits you and the needs of your class.

There is a tick box next to each workout on the contents page. Use this to record which workouts have been attempted. You can also use the progress charts to track pupils' confidence.

Contents — Autumn Term

- ☐ Workout 1 2
  - The alphabet
- ☐ Workout 2 4
  - Capital letters and numbers
- ☐ Workout 3 6
  - The first join
- ☐ Workout 4 8
  - The second join
- ☐ Workout 5 10
  - The third join
- ☐ Workout 6 12
  - The fourth join
- ☐ Workout 7 14
  - The fifth join
- ☐ Workout 8 16
  - The sixth join
- ☐ Workout 9 18
  - Joining to e
- ☐ Workout 10 20
  - Break letters
- ☐ Workout 11 22
  - Capital letters recap
- ☐ Workout 12 24
  - Joining with e, f and s
  - Break letters

Contents — Autumn Term

- ☑ **Workout 1** 2
  - The alphabet
- ☑ **Workout 2** 4
  - Capital letters and numbers
- ☑ **Workout 3** 6
  - The first join
- ☑ **Workout 4** 8
  - The second join
- ☑ **Workout 5** 10
  - The third join
- ☑ **Workout 6** 12
  - The fourth join
- ☑ **Workout 7** 14
  - The fifth join
- ☑ **Workout 8** 16
  - The sixth join
- ☑ **Workout 9** 18
  - Joining to e
- ☑ **Workout 10** 20
  - Break letters
- ☑ **Workout 11** 22
  - Capital letters recap
- ☑ **Workout 12** 24
  - Joining with e, f and s
  - Break letters

Contents — Spring Term

- [ ] **Workout 1** 26
  - The first, second and third joins
- [ ] **Workout 2** 28
  - The fourth, fifth and sixth joins
- [ ] **Workout 3** 30
  - Joining with f and e
  - Break letters
- [ ] **Workout 4** 32
  - Tricky words
- [ ] **Workout 5** 34
  - Words ending in 'ge' and 'dge'
- [ ] **Workout 6** 36
  - Words ending in 'le', 'al', 'el' and 'il'
- [ ] **Workout 7** 38
  - Words with the soft 'c' sound
- [ ] **Workout 8** 40
  - Words with silent letters
- [ ] **Workout 9** 42
  - Words with the hard 'c' sound
- [ ] **Workout 10** 44
  - Words with the 'ur' sound
- [ ] **Workout 11** 46
  - The suffixes 'ed', 'ing', 'er' and 'est'
- [ ] **Workout 12** 48
  - Words with the 'igh' sound

Contents — Summer Term

☑ **Workout 1** 50
  • Words with the 'or' sound

☑ **Workout 2** 52
  • Words ending in 'ey'

☑ **Workout 3** 54
  • Plurals

☑ **Workout 4** 56
  • Words with the short 'o' sound

☑ **Workout 5** 58
  • The suffixes 'ly', 'ness', 'ful', 'less' and 'ment'

☑ **Workout 6** 60
  • Words ending in 'tion'

☑ **Workout 7** 62
  • Contractions

☑ **Workout 8** 64
  • Homophones

☑ **Workout 9** 66
  • Tricky words

☑ **Workout 10** 68
  • Beach-themed words and sentences

☑ **Workout 11** 70
  • Fantasy-themed words and sentences

☑ **Workout 12** 72
  • Rainforest-themed words and sentences

Progress Charts 74

Autumn Term: Workout 1

Warm up

1. Trace these letters. The blue dots show you where to start.

   a b c d

Now try these:

2. Trace these letters, then copy them. Start at the dot each time.

   e f g h

   i j k l

   m n o p

   q r s t

   u v w

x y z

Challenge: Magical Mayhem!

Felipe has a recipe for a spell, but some of the words are jumbled up. Unscramble each set of letters in blue, then add them to the sentences to find out what he needs.

a dozen chilled *bast*
feiv jumpy pink squids
six *crwo* wings

a dozen chilled

jumpy pink squids

six   wings

Can you spot all the letters of the alphabet?

Challenge Complete?

Is your handwriting enchanting?

Autumn Term: Workout 2

Warm up

1. Trace these capital letters and numbers. Start at the blue dots.

Now try these:

2. Trace these names, then copy them out underneath. Start each name at the blue dot.

3. Trace the address, then copy it out underneath.

4. Now copy out these place names twice.

Tokyo

Greece

Peru

Challenge: Postal Problems!

Mila wants to send some letters, but the postcodes haven't been written properly. Write out the postcodes correctly using capital letters and numbers. The first one has been done for you.

b i five   six h e

BI5 6HE

f a three   eight k d

Challenge Complete? ✓

Did you do a first class job?

Autumn Term: Workout 3

Warm up

1. These pairs of letters are connected by the first join. Trace each pair twice, starting at the blue dot each time.

   an   *ep*   *di*   *ty*

   an   *ep*   *di*   *ty*

Now try these:

2. Now trace these pairs of letters, then copy them out.

   ai   ai   ai

   ew   ew   ew

   cr   cr   cr

   lm   lm   lm

3. First trace these words, then copy them out.

him   *dip*

cup   *tiny*

mummy

Challenge: Exploration Station!

Akwasi is going on an adventure. Write the first letter of each thing that Akwasi sees. Make sure you join it properly to the next letter.

 izard      ushroom

 ill

Challenge Complete?

How was your handwriting adventure?

Autumn Term: Workout 4

Warm up

1. Trace these pairs of letters that all use the second join. Start at the blue dot each time.

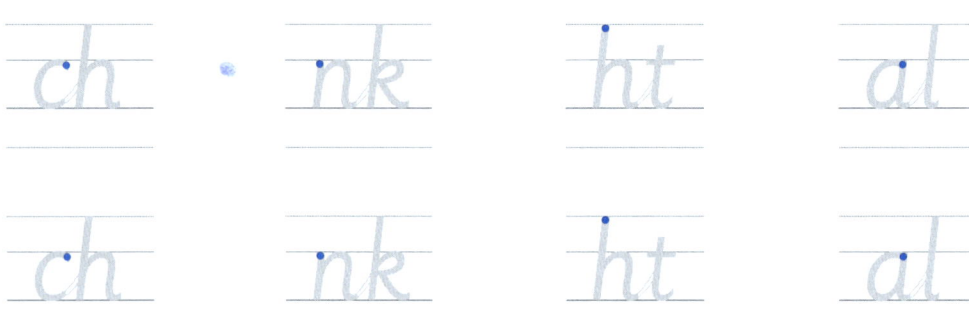

Now try these:

2. Trace these letters, then copy them out.

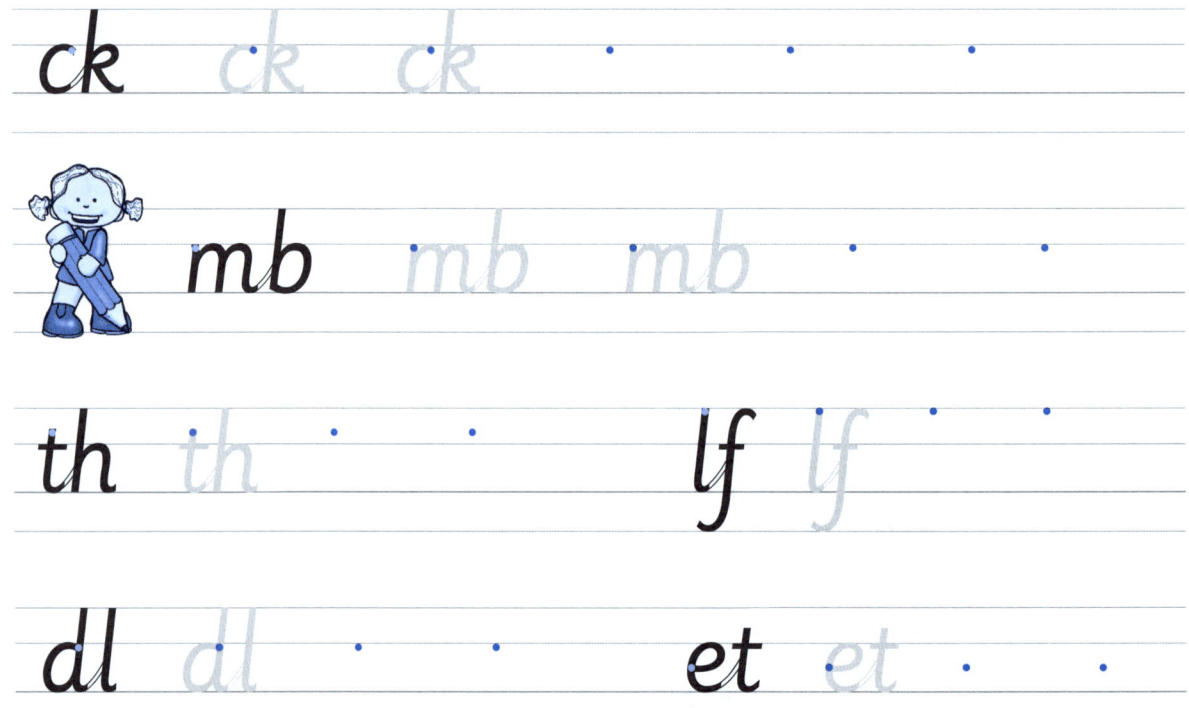

3. Now trace these words, then copy them out underneath.

all   tub   milk   chill

club   chunk   tilt

Challenge: Forest Fun!

Lily spotted some things in the forest. She wrote them down, but she got the letters mixed up. Unscramble the letters to make a word that matches the picture.

atn   *tun*

Challenge Complete? ✓

Do you feel jolly about joining?

Autumn Term: Workout 5

Warm up

1. These pairs of letters are connected by the third join.
   Trace each pair, starting at the blue dot each time.

Now try these:

2. Trace these letters, then copy them out.

   dg *dg* · · · ·

   iq *iq* · *ic* *ic* ·

3. These pairs of letters all use the third join to **s**.
   Trace the pairs, then copy them out.

4. Now trace these words, then copy them out underneath.

mad   dig   has   undo

lacks   land   muddy

Challenge: Farm Friends!

Can you label all of the animals on the farm? Write the names of each one on the lines, using the upside down words to help you.

cat

duck

lamb

Challenge Complete? ✓

Were you baa-rilliant at those pages?

Autumn Term: Workout 6

Warm up

1. These pairs of letters are connected by the fourth join. Trace each pair, starting at the blue dot each time.

   rn   vi   ou   wr

   rn   vi   ou   wr

Now try these:

2. Trace these letters, then copy them out.

   op   op

   rm   rm

3. Trace and copy these letter pairs that use the fourth join from **f**. You'll have to lift your pencil off the page to make the join.

   fr   fi   fy

4. Now trace these words, then copy them out underneath.

run   own   fib   toy

evil   corn   furry

Challenge: Bandwriting!

Amaya has written down all the instruments she can play. Can you write each one underneath its picture?

Challenge Complete?

Did you hit the right note?

Autumn Term: Workout 7

Warm up

1. These pairs of letters are connected by the fifth join.
   Trace them, starting at the blue dot each time.

   oh   rl   wt   rf
   oh   rl   wt   rf

Now try these:

2. Trace these letter pairs, then copy them out.

   ob   ob   ob

   rh   rh   rh

   wk   wk   wk

   ff   ff   ff

3. Now trace these words, then copy them out.

fluffy *howl*

lift *early*

cliff *hourly*

Challenge: Zany Zoo!

All of the labels for the animal enclosures have been written in capital letters. Rewrite them on the lines using joined-up lowercase letters.

HAWK

RHINO

MOTH

OWL

Challenge Complete?

Was that a roaring success?

Autumn Term: Workout 8

Warm up

1. Trace these pairs of letters. They're all connected by the sixth join. Don't forget to start at the blue dot each time.

oc   rg   wd   oq

oc   rg   wd   oq

Now try these:

2. Trace these pairs of letters, then copy them out.

oa   oa   oa

fo   fo   fo

va   va   va

fs   fs   fs

3. Now trace these phrases, then copy them out.

thick fog

rainfall

warm day

Challenge: Menu Mix-up!

Geoff the waiter has made a list of things he needs to fetch from the kitchen. Copy them out on the lines in joined-up writing.

Challenge Complete? ✓

Were those pages a piece of cake?

Autumn Term: Workout 9

Warm up

1. These pairs of letters all include a join to **e**.
   Trace each pair of letters, starting at the blue dot each time.

Now try these:

2. Trace these pairs of letters, then copy them out.

3. Now trace the **ee** join, then copy it out.

4. Trace these phrases, then copy them out.
   Remember to start each word at the blue dot.

a meadow

red flower

leafy trees

Challenge: Space Race!

Zippo wants to know some facts about a race in space. However, her computer has put all the letters backwards. Rewrite the answers so the letters are in the right order.

Who won the race?

neila na

What did they fly?

tekcor a

Challenge Complete?

Is your handwriting out of this world?

Autumn Term: Workout 10

Warm up

1. All the words below start with break letters.
   Trace them all, starting from the blue dot each time.

Now try these:

2. Trace these words that start with break letters.
   Then, copy them out underneath.

3. Trace these words, then copy them out underneath.
   Each word has a break letter in the middle.

4. Trace and copy the words below, starting at the blue dot. Each word has more than one break letter in it.

jungle

toybox

squeeze

Challenge: A Scary Situation!

Harry was so frightened in the haunted house that he muddled up these words. Unscramble the letters in each word, then write them on the lines.

spokoy

piders

hgost

obo

Challenge Complete? ✓

Was your handwriting scarily good?

Autumn Term: Workout 11

Warm up

1. Trace these names. Start at the blue dot each time.

Now try these:

2. Trace these place names, then copy them underneath.

3. Trace the day and the months. Then, copy them underneath.

4. Trace the sentence, then copy it out underneath.

Dr Liu speaks Arabic.

Challenge: A Soaring Sentence?

Iman has written a sentence, but the capital letters are in the wrong places. Read Iman's sentence below, then rewrite it so it uses capital letters correctly. Start each new word at the dot.

i Will go To braziL with pEdro In octoBer.

Challenge Complete?

Did you fly through these pages?

Autumn Term: Workout 12

Warm up

1. These words include joins to **e**. Trace them, starting at the dot.

   nine   bread   bee

Now try these:

2. These words include joins with **f**.
   Trace them, then copy them out underneath.

   flag   coffee   fifty   safari

3. These words all include the letter **s**.
   Trace them, then copy them out underneath.

   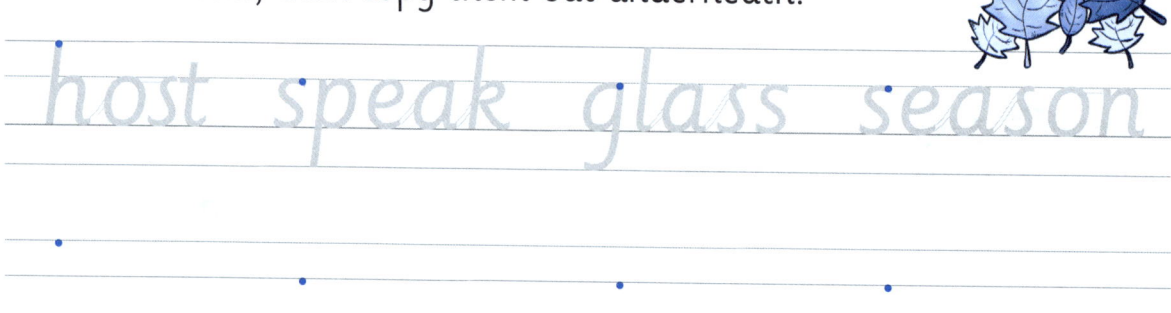

   host   speak   glass   season

4. Trace these phrases, then copy them out.
   They both include break letters.

   six pizzas

   gobble jelly

   ### Challenge: Rowdy Robots!

   Ifama's robot is making a huge mess. Fill in the gaps in the instructions using the words in the box to help her turn it off.

   | button | press | biggest |

   You must   the

   Which button should Ifama press? Circle it.

   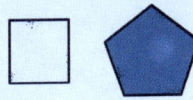  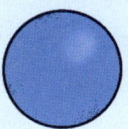   **Challenge Complete?**

Bleep bleep! How did you find that?

Spring Term: Workout 1

Warm up

1. Trace these pairs of letters. Start at the blue dot each time.

Now try these:

2. Trace these words that contain the first join, then copy them out.

3. Trace these words that contain the second join, then copy them.

4. Trace these words that contain the third join, then copy them out underneath.

ear tag land licking

Challenge: Fairy Fun!

Fatima the fairy has dropped some words and all the letters have got mixed up. Unscramble the letters and write the words out using joined-up writing.

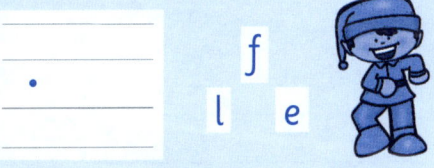

Challenge Complete?

Is your handwriting magical?

Spring Term: Workout 2

Warm up

1. Trace these pairs of letters. Start at the blue dot each time.

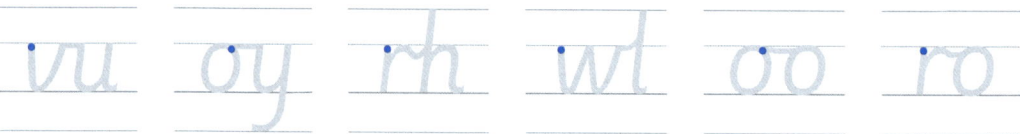

Now try these:

2. Trace these words that contain the fourth join, then copy them out underneath. Start each word at the dot.

firm   rich   witch   fiction

3. Trace these words, then copy them. They all contain the fifth join.

why   curl   violin   muffin

4. Trace these words that contain the sixth join, then copy them.

fact   wrong   claws

Challenge: Castle Conundrum!

Jasmine is exploring an old castle, but she's lost. To help her get out, use the words in the box to fill the gaps in the sentence.

| four | with | old | arrows |

Go in the   door

                    on it.

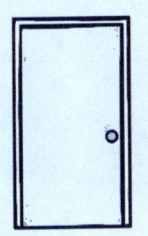  

Which door should Jasmine choose? Circle it.

Challenge Complete?

How was your handwriting this time?

Spring Term: Workout 2

Spring Term: Workout 3

Warm up

1. Trace these pairs of letters, starting at the blue dot each time.

   fi   ft   ke   oe   pi   su

Now try these:

2. Trace these words with **f** joins, then copy them out underneath.

   flour   fruit   follow   whiff

3. Trace these words that use joins to **e**, then copy them.

   tree   more   throne   lettuce

4. Trace these words with break letters, then copy them out.

jogs   sixty   blaze

Challenge: Commotion in the Ocean!

The names of these sea creatures have all been written without any joins. Rewrite them using joined-up handwriting.

starfish

lobster

dolphin

squid

Challenge Complete? ✓

Did you have a whale of a time?

Spring Term: Workout 4

Warm up

1. Trace these tricky words. Start at the blue dot each time.

Now try these:

2. Trace these words, then copy them out underneath. Remember to start each word at the blue dot.

3. Copy these words. Start each word at the blue dot.

hold   pass   sure   find

4. Now trace the phrases, then copy them out.

whole class

every child

Challenge: Charming Cupcakes!

Mr Mazari works in a cupcake shop.
Use the words in the box to finish these sentences.

> pretty
> sugar
> busy

I have been _____ today.

Where is the _____ ?

That one looks _____ .

Challenge Complete?

Yum! How did that go?

Spring Term: Workout 5

Warm up

1. Trace these words. Start each word at the blue dot.

Now try these:

2. These words all end in **ge**.
   Trace the words, then copy them out underneath.

   page　　*sausage*　　*sponge*

3. These words all end in **dge**.
   Trace the words, then copy them out underneath.

   judge　　*dodge*　　*fudge*

4. Now copy these phrases that contain the soft **g** sound.

magic gem

good genie

Challenge: Artistic Antics!

Leo labelled all his artwork. However, he wrote all the labels in capital letters. Fix Leo's labels by writing the words in lowercase joined-up letters.

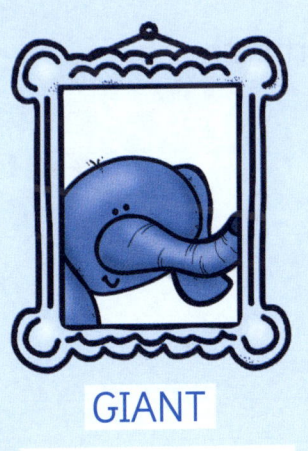

SMUDGE

ORANGE

GIANT

Challenge Complete?

Is your handwriting a work of art?

Spring Term: Workout 6

Warm up

1. These words end **le**, **al**, **il** and **el**.
   Trace them, starting each word at the blue dot.

 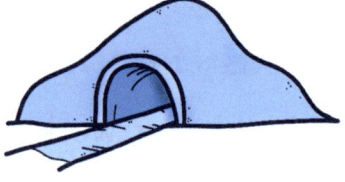

Now try these:

2. Trace these words, then copy them out underneath.

3. Now copy these words.

icicle   camel   medal

Challenge: What's in the School Bag?

Asami's school bag is full of useful things for the classroom. Using joined-up handwriting, label the objects in the bag.

Challenge Complete?

Is your handwriting top of the class?

Spring Term: Workout 7

Warm up

1. These words all contain the soft **c** sound. Trace them, starting at the blue dot each time.

Now try these:

2. Trace these words, then copy them out underneath. Start each word at the blue dot.

   once   dance   voice   cymbal

3. Copy these words. Start each word at the blue dot.

   circle   parcel   cycle   decide

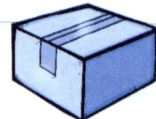

4. Copy these phrases.

fancy mice

nice prince

palace ball

Challenge: Messy Map!

All the labels in Aaliyah's map are upside down. Rewrite them so they're the right way up. Don't forget to use joined-up writing.

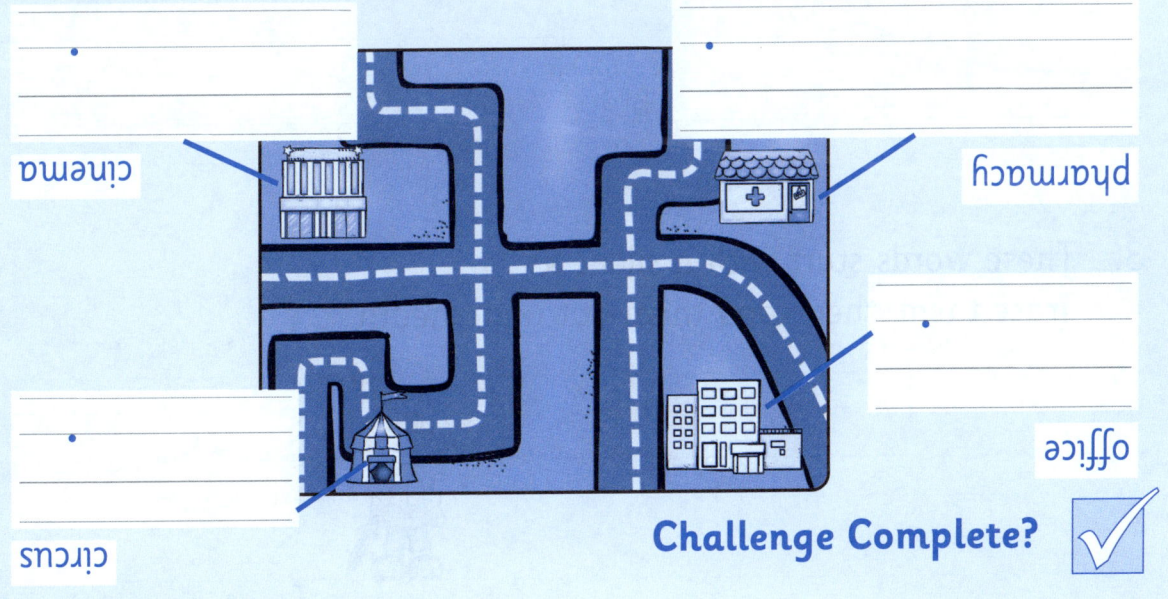

Challenge Complete?

Did you dance through those pages?

Spring Term: Workout 8

Warm up

1. Trace these words with silent letters, starting at the blue dot.

Now try these:

2. These words include a silent **g**.
   Trace them, then copy them out underneath.

3. These words start with a silent **k**.
   Trace them, then copy them out underneath.

4. These words all start with a silent **w**. Copy them out.

write   wriggle   wrong

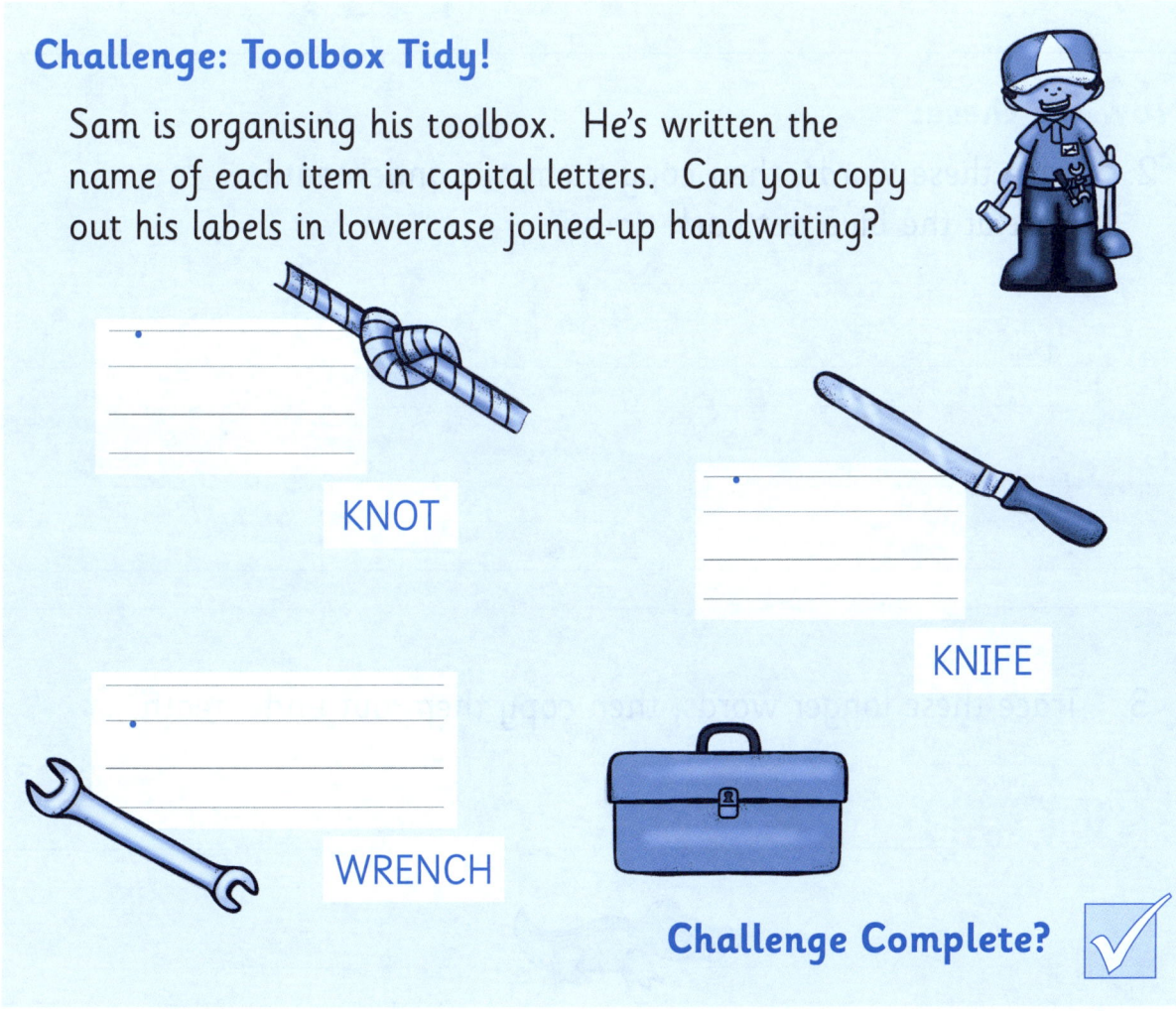

Challenge: Toolbox Tidy!

Sam is organising his toolbox. He's written the name of each item in capital letters. Can you copy out his labels in lowercase joined-up handwriting?

KNOT

KNIFE

WRENCH

Challenge Complete?

Did you nail those pages?

Spring Term: Workout 9

Warm up

1. These words all contain the hard **c** sound.
   Trace them, starting at the blue dot each time.

   kite   *cost*   *rock*

Now try these:

2. Trace these words, then copy them out underneath.
   Start at the blue dot each time.

   bike carrot block koala

3. Trace these longer words, then copy them out underneath.

   crocodile   continent

4. Now copy this phrase.

a locket in a coat pocket

Challenge: Crazy Kangaroo!

Finish the sentences by using the words in the box to fill in the blanks. Remember to write in joined-up handwriting.

clapped   kangaroo   crown

A _____ played kazoo for the king. He _____ and gave her a _____.

Challenge Complete?

Are you feeling cool and confident?

Spring Term: Workout 10

Warm up

1. Trace these words that use the **ur** sound.
   Start each word at the blue dot.

Now try these:

2. Trace these words, then copy them out underneath.
   Start at the blue dot each time.

   burn   twirl   work   herd

3. Copy these words.

   world   skirt   burger

4. Copy this phrase. Remember to start each word at the blue dot.

Shirley's purple turkey

Challenge: Wonderful Wildlife!

Ramona has made a list of the wildlife she has seen around the river, but she's written the words upside down. Rewrite the words so that they are the right way up.

bird

worm

turtle

otter

Challenge Complete?

Did that go swimmingly?

Spring Term: Workout 11

Warm up

1. Trace these suffixes. Start at the blue dot each time.

Now try these:

2. Trace these words, then copy them out.

3. Copy these words, starting at the blue dot each time.

cared   *caring*

nicer   *nicest*

4. Now copy these words.

swimming

thinnest

Challenge: Running Race!

Rachel and Rob had a race. Their friend wrote some sentences about it in mirror writing. Rewrite the sentences the right way round, then circle who you think won the race.

Rob was running quickly.

Rachel was the fastest.

Challenge Complete?

Is your handwriting a winner?

Spring Term: Workout 12

Warm up

1. Trace these words that use the **igh** sound.
   Start at the blue dot each time.

Now try these:

2. Trace these words, then copy them out underneath.

3. Copy these words.

   might   untie   bite   try

4. Now copy this phrase.

a pie high in the sky

Challenge: Plant Power!

Pietro is listing some things that plants need to grow. Use the words in the box to complete Pietro's phrases.

light
right
supply

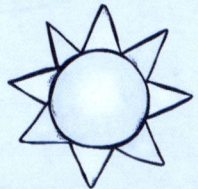 *from the sun*

the   temperature

 *a good water*

Challenge Complete?

Was that as easy as pie?

Summer Term: Workout 1

Warm up

1. Trace these words with the **or** sound.
   Start each word at the blue dot.

Now try these:

2. Trace these words, then copy them out underneath.
   Start each word at the blue dot.

   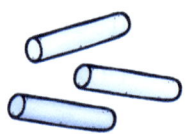

   all   chalk   award   ignore

3. Copy out these words on the lines underneath,
   starting at the blue dot each time.

4. Copy the sentence.

Tall horses walk slowly.

Challenge: Wonderful Wordsearch!

Find the four words in the box in the wordsearch.
Write each word on the lines next to the correct picture.

| wardrobe | small | north | eyeball |

Challenge Complete? ✓

How did you find those pages?

© CGP — not to be photocopied

Summer Term: Workout 1

Summer Term: Workout 2

Warm up

1. Trace these words ending in **ey**. Start at the blue dot each time.

Now try these:

2. Trace these words, then copy them out underneath.

3. Copy this sentence. Start each word at the dot.

Look at that deep valley.

4. Now copy these phrases.

sad monkey

fast donkey

Challenge: Speedy Shopping!

Use the items on the right to fill in the shopping list.

Shopping List

1.
2.
3.

1.
   trolley

2.
   honey

3.
   turkey

One of the items on the list isn't something you can take home from the shop. Can you spot which one? Circle it.

Challenge Complete?

Do you have super handwriting skills?

Summer Term: Workout 3

Warm up

1. Trace these plural words. Start each word at the blue dot.

worms   puppies   boxes

Now try these:

2. Trace these words, then copy them out underneath.

bins   lorries   ostriches

3. Copy these phrases, starting each word at the blue dot.

sour limes

ripe berries

4. Now copy out this sentence.

The ponies had parties.

Challenge: Lost in the Library!

Luke the librarian has mixed up the letters of the bookshelf labels. Unscramble the letters to show what the books are about. You can use the book covers to help you.

sipes

bsabie

sprost

twiches

Challenge Complete? ✓

Were those pages a fairy tale?

Summer Term: Workout 4

Warm up

1. Trace these words that contain the short **o** sound.

Now try these:

2. Trace these words, then copy them out underneath. Start each word at the blue dot.

3. Copy these words.

squash   washes   popcorn

4. Now copy this sentence.

The swan has a wallet.

Challenge: Marvellous Mermaid!

Molly the mermaid wants to go home to her cave, but there are obstacles in her way. Label the dangers using the words in the box, then draw a safe path.

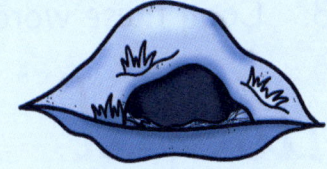

fog
rocks
swamp

Challenge Complete?

Have you mer-made a big effort?

Summer Term: Workout 5

Warm up

1. These words all end with suffixes.
   Trace them, starting at the blue dot each time.

Now try these:

2. Trace these words, then copy them out underneath.

3. Copy these words. Start at the blue dot each time.

   useful   bubbly   payment

4. Now copy this sentence.

Her kindness is limitless.

Challenge: A Round of Applause!

Billy the dancer's performance has been reviewed in a local newspaper, but some of the words have been printed backwards. Copy out the words the right way round.

It was such a lufyoj show.

I watched in tnemezama.

I will ylniatrec go again.

Challenge Complete? ✓

Does your writing get a good review?

Summer Term: Workout 6

Warm up

1. These words all end in **tion**.
   Trace them, starting at the blue dot.

   nation   fiction   motion

Now try these:

2. Trace these words, then copy them on the lines underneath.

   action   caution   narration

3. Now copy these words.
   Start each word at the blue dot.

   question   emotion   station

4. Now copy this phrase.

a portion of the potion

Challenge: Maths Muddle!

These maths words have been jumbled up. Using the symbols to help, unscramble the letters and write out the words using joined-up handwriting.

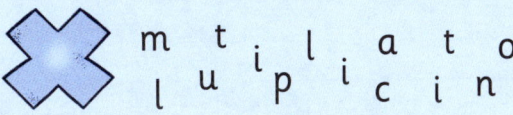

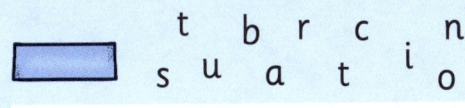

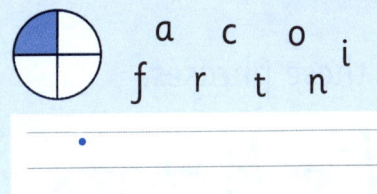

Challenge Complete?

Is your handwriting one in a million?

Summer Term: Workout 7

Warm up

1. These words are all contractions.
   Trace them, starting each word at the blue dot.

Now try these:

2. Trace and copy these words. Start at the blue dot each time.

3. Copy these phrases.

   bird's boots

   horse's hat

4. Now copy this sentence.

Kai's corgis can't bark.

Challenge: Halil's Holiday!

Halil is going on holiday. Copy out these sentences to help him remember what to do at the airport. Use joined-up handwriting.

You mustn't forget your passport.

Make sure your suitcase isn't too heavy.

Challenge Complete? ✓

Was that a soaring success?

Summer Term: Workout 8

Warm up

1. Trace these pairs of homophones.
   Start each word at the blue dot.

Now try these:

2. Trace and copy these pairs of homophones.
   Start at the blue dot each time.

   raise   rays

   bear   bare

3. Copy these words.

   their   there   they're

4. Now copy this sentence.

She stares at the stairs.

Challenge: Pesky Pairs!

Each of these pictures shows a pair of homophones. Write down the missing word from each pair. Use joined-up writing.

 *night*

 *flour*

 *hare*

Challenge Complete?

How do you feel after those pages?

Summer Term: Workout 9

Warm up

1. Trace these tricky words. Start at the blue dot each time.

Now try these:

2. Trace and copy these words.

3. Copy these words.

beautiful   everybody

4. Now copy this sentence.

I only wear gold clothes.

Challenge: Gorgeous Garden!

Gregory's friends are helping him with his garden. Fill in the gaps in his to-do list using the words in the box. Use the pictures to help you.

> grass
> Water
> Plant

_____ the flowers.

 *_____ the seeds.*

Mow the _____.

Challenge Complete?

Is your handwriting blossoming?

Summer Term: Workout 10

Warm up

1. Trace these beach-themed words. Start at the blue dot.

Now try these:

2. Trace these sentences, then copy them out underneath. Start each sentence at the blue dot.

Don't step on the seaweed.

It's slippy, slimy and wet.

3. Copy these phrases.

seagull egg

rough sand

salty waves

Challenge: Silly Shells!

Pavel has written some sentences about things he found at the beach, but some of the words have been jumbled up. Unscramble the words in blue and copy them out using joined-up handwriting.

| This shell is wdie. | The crab is psotyt. | This shell is siwrly. |

 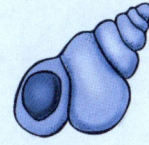

Challenge Complete?

Were those pages a ray of sunshine?

Summer Term: Workout 11

Warm up

1. Trace these words. Start at the blue dot each time.

   blaze   roar   mighty

   flame   spark

Now try these:

2. Trace and copy these sentences. Start each line at the blue dot.

   People thought the dragon

   didn't like the princess.

They were really friends.

Challenge: Jazzy Jewels!

These words have all been written without any joins. Rewrite them using joined-up handwriting.

dazzle

priceless

valuable

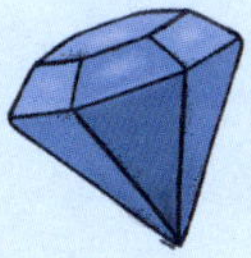

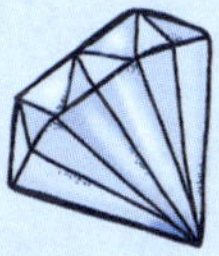

sparkling

polished

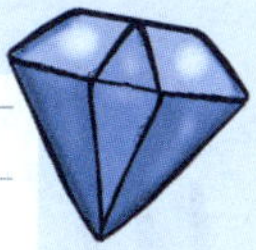

Challenge Complete? ✓

Does your handwriting sparkle?

Summer Term: Workout 12

Warm up

1. Trace these words about the rainforest.

Now try these:

2. Copy these sentences. Start each line at the blue dot.

Animals like lemurs and

toucans live in rainforests.

There are butterflies too.

Challenge: Rumble in the Jungle!

The words in these sentences have been jumbled up and now they don't make sense. Put the words in the right order and write out the full sentences.

| trees from Sloths hang. |

| flap their Parrots wings. |

Challenge Complete?

Are you wild about handwriting?

Autumn Term — Progress Chart

Fill in the progress chart after you finish each workout.

Tick the box under the face that shows how you feel.

	😕	🙂	😉
Workout 1			
Workout 2			
Workout 3			
Workout 4			
Workout 5			
Workout 6			
Workout 7			
Workout 8			
Workout 9			
Workout 10			
Workout 11			
Workout 12			

Progress Chart

Spring Term — Progress Chart

Fill in the progress chart after you finish each workout.

Tick the box under the face that shows how you feel.

	😐	🙂	😉
Workout 1			
Workout 2			
Workout 3			
Workout 4			
Workout 5			
Workout 6			
Workout 7			
Workout 8			
Workout 9			
Workout 10			
Workout 11			
Workout 12			

Progress Chart

Summer Term — Progress Chart

Fill in the progress chart after you finish each workout.

Tick the box under the face that shows how you feel.

	😐	🙂	😉
Workout 1			
Workout 2			
Workout 3			
Workout 4			
Workout 5			
Workout 6			
Workout 7			
Workout 8			
Workout 9			
Workout 10			
Workout 11			
Workout 12			